EL ESCORIAL

Editorial Everest, S. A., wish to thank all members of the National Heritage who have so kindly collaborated in the production of this book.

Photography: Oronoz
Everest Archives

2 nd EDITION

© EDITORIAL EVEREST, S. A.
Ctra. León-La Coruña, km 5 - LEÓN
ISBN: 84-241-4966-1
Legal deposit: LE: 1050-1991
Printed in Spain

EDITORIAL EVERGRÁFICAS, S. A.
Ctra. León-La Coruña, km 5
LEÓN (Spain)
Produced in collaboration with the National Heritage.

EL ESCORIAL
ROYAL MONASTERY OF SAN LORENZO

JUAN LOSADA – JOSÉ MANUEL TORNERO

Editorial Everest, S. A.

MADRID • LEON • BARCELONA • SEVILLA • GRANADA • VALENCIA
ZARAGOZA • LAS PALMAS DE GRAN CANARIA • LA CORUÑA
PALMA DE MALLORCA • ALICANTE – MEXICO • BUENOS AIRES

1. *Felipe II's seat in La Herrería wood;
from here the king would watch the
construction of the monastery.*

HISTORICAL INTRODUCTION

It can be said that the Royal Monastery of San Lorenzo (St. Laurence) in El Escorial, known as the eighth wonder of the world, and declared a Monument of World Interest by the United Nations Organization (UNO), is a work of universal dimension.

The monument is superintended by the National Heritage Organization, which takes care of its management and administration, as well as the custody and conservation of its funds.

This Royal Monastery was founded by Felipe II as an act of thanks for the victory of San Quintín, when in 1557 the Spanish army conquered the French on 10th August, the feast day of St. Laurence. At the same time he was fulfilling his father, Emperor V's wish that a pantheon should be constructed for his remains, and for those of his descendents.

From among various options, the site chosen was a hill just outside the small town of El Escorial, where there was abundant water and pleasant scenery. The foundation was carried out by the Hieronymite Order, chosen basically for its Spanish origins, and also because this was the order that had accompanied Carlos V in Yuste.

Felipe II's secretary, Pedro de Hoyo, and his chief architect, Juan Bautista de Toledo, held preparatory meetings in the nearby towns of Galapagar and Guadarrama with Juan de Huete and Juan de Colmenar, who had been named prior and vicar respectively of the new monastery. They finally decided on the works which were to take twenty-one years to finish — from 1563 to 1584.

The preparations began in 1562. In the same year the organisers were joined by Antonio de Villacastín, a Hieronymite brother who was to become one of the central figures in the work. He was an intimate collaborator with the architects in the construction. The first stone was laid on 23rd April 1563.

The death of Juan Bautista de Toledo in 1567 did not lead to an interruption in the work, as Juan de Herrera, assistant to the first architect, immediately took over.

The building grew quickly, and in 1573 and 1574 the first bodies were taken to the monastery. Among them were those of Emperor Carlos V and Empress Isabel. The foundations of the main church were laid in 1575. In 1576 the marble crucifix by Benvenuto Cellini was taken there from El Pardo palace.

The last stone was finally laid on 13th September 1584, in the presence of Felipe II. The church was inaugurated on 9th August 1586. Those monarchs who had up to then been laid to rest in the *Prestado* or *Old* Church later passed to the high altar in this church.

2. *General view of El Escorial Monastery from the North-west corner.*

THE OUTSIDE OF EL ESCORIAL MONASTERY

On the North and West sides the building appears to be surrounded by the portico, limited by a thick stone wall, the gates of which are tied with chains, and on the South and East sides, by beautiful gardens. The houses of the Offices, Ministries, Princes and Queens, as well as those of the Order of Monks are placed around the portico. All constructed in stone, they are in keeping with the style of the monastery.

The work itself is made up of a rectangular parallelogram of 207 by 161 metres; in the four corners are towers of 55 metres with spires topped with balls supporting a weather vane and a cross. Worthy of mention are the twin bell towers, measuring 72

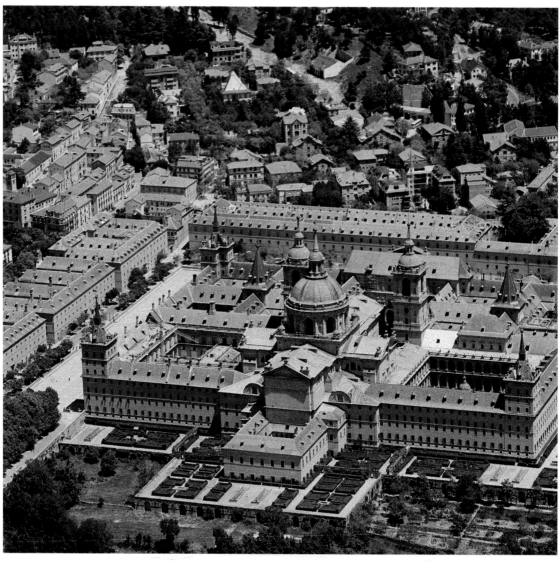

3. *General view of the monastery from the East.*

4. *The North and West Façades.*

metres each; the magnificent dome is at a height of 92 metres.

Due to the difference in the character and direction of the façades, they will be dealt with separately.

The West Façade

This is the main façade. It is 207 metres long by 20 high; the towers on either side are 55 metres high. A cornice runs along it at a height of some 17 metres, dividing it into two parts. The lower part is Doric, and the upper Ionic; this is topped with a triangular pediment with acroterium and balls. The main door is set in the centre of this façade. Measuring three metres wide by six high, it is adorned by four columns with niches and windows, and in the upper part by a window with wrought-iron work on the sides. In the central part of the second section is a statue of St. Laurence and below it Felipe II's royal coat of arms, both by Juan Bautista Monegro.

The South Façade

Measuring 161 metres long and with 296 windows, this façade is not inferior to the West façade.

9

5. *The main doorway, in the centre of the West, or portico, façade.*

6. *A view of the central core of the monastery:*
the main entrance, the King's Courtyard, the basilica.

For it to reach the level of the portico a buttress of five metres has been added over the terrace of the gardens. The most notable aspect of this façade is its complete simplicity. It contains four rows of windows and three small doors — one in each tower and one in the middle.

The most beautiful garden is on this façade; known as the Monk's Garden,

it offers some views of the Guadarrama.

The beauty of this façade is further increased by the Convalescents' Gallery, which was used by convalescents to take a walk, as from here they could enjoy both the air from the mountains and a magnificent view of them. Made up of two parts, the lower being Doric and the upper Ionic, it is by Juan de Herrera.

7. *The South Façade; the pond and the Monks' Garden.* ▶

8. *Detail of one of the towers.*

dorned frontispiece, which is the back of the main chapel. A square tower at each end completes the façade.

The Dome

Rising up from the basilica, it has a circumference of 83 metres. It dominates the whole monastery. In the drum are eight windows of almost ten metres in height; a wide cornice with a beautiful balustrade runs right round the dome. The dome has eight windows, each of five metres; rising up from the small cupola there is a stone spire topped with a bronze ball; on this there is an iron cross which measures two metres in height.

9. *The dome seen from the East.*

The North Façade

161 metres long, it contains 180 windows. It is divided into sections by pilasters, between which there are four rows of windows; it contains three large doorways. There is a very small fourth doorway in the Ladies' Tower, which was used by Felipe II as the former main stairway to the palace was close to it.

The West Façade

This is the simplest of all. It contains 386 windows, which are divided into five rows. In the central part is a plain, una-

10. *The six Kings of Judea on the façade of the basilica, in the Kings' Courtyard.*

THE KINGS' COURTYARD

This courtyard receives its name from the six large statues of the kings of Judea on the façade of the church. Five metres tall, they are by J. B. Monegro in granite and marble, the materials he also employed for his statue of St. Laurence. The crowns, sceptres and insignia, in gilded bronze, are by S. Fernández; the inscriptions beside each of the statues were affixed in 1660.

The courtyard is 64 metres long by 38 wide, and has four rows of windows, with a total of 80 on each side. On the left-hand wall, looking towards the basilica, between the eighth and the ninth windows is the last stone to be laid in the building. It is marked by a small black cross. Another larger one, formed by the cut of the slate, can be seen above it, on the roof.

11. *View of the Kings' courtyard; in the background the façade of the basilica.*

12. *A ceremony in the Kings' courtyard. Print by Brambilla, 19th century.* ▶

THE BASILICA

Raised on a large platform, which is reached by seven steps, it is Doric in style and comprises two sections with a tower at each end. The lower section is made up of alternate columns and arches, with wide balconies; the upper section, divided from the lower one by a cornice, is made up of six large pedestals, which are supported by the half columns in the lower section. It is topped with a wide frontispiece with a window giving onto the choir in the church.

The towers reach a height of 72 metres and end in a pyramidal spike of stone, crowned, as in other parts of the building, with a metal ball with a cross and a weather vane.

Just inside the building is the hallway of the church, with a vault supported by ten arches corresponding to those on the exterior. There is a door in each of the arches; the three central doors lead to the church itself. On the sides are two black marble medallions. The inscription on one alludes to the laying of the first stone of the church and the beginning of the masses in the vigil to St. Laurence, and on the other to the consecration of the basilica.

The framework of the doors is of excellent wood, and the floorboards are of holm oak. All the doors lead to the vestibule of the church, or the lower choir. Square in shape, it contains four chapels and an unusual vault which in spite of its length appears to be flat.

Finally, from the archways of the seminaries the church can be entered through a large door with a bronze grille, which was wrought and gilded in Zaragoza, in the Tujarón workshop, as were the other four matching doors.

The church is square in shape, measuring some 50 metres on each side, and is predominantly Doric in style, with a layout similar to that of St. Peter's in Rome. Four large central buttresses support the dome on pendentives. The dome reaches a height of 92 metres. 24 arches which support the vaults rest on another eight pillars, opposite the buttresses. In the part towards the lesser aisles the buttresses appear to be pierced through by two spaces ending in a round arch. In the lower aisle there are several small altars, and in the upper part a gallery leading nowhere.

The vaults, which are made of brick, were formerly of stucco, except those over the main altar and the choir, which were painted by Lucas Cambiaso (Luchetto); during the reign of Carlos II the stucco work was replaced by frescoes by Lucas Jordán.

The basilica receives light through a total of 38 windows. The floor is paved in alternate white and grey slabs of marble, in keeping with the profound sobriety of the decoration as a whole.

Worthy of note are the paintings on the altars which represent, in groups of two, the most important male and female saints, together with their different attributes. The most important of the painters of these saints is Juan Fernández de Navarrete (nicknamed the Dumb Painter), who produced a remarkable group of apostles on six canvases.

13. Nave of the basilica, with the dome and the main altar. ▶

14. *The altarpiece at the high altar.*

The main chapel is a continuation of the central nave of the church. It is separated from it by a large arch on heavy pillars and, at floor level, twelve marble steps. Beyond these steps is the choir, with a marble and jasper floor in several colours. At the sides are the oratories and the royal tombs. Five more steps lead up to a second platform where the high altar is placed. Also made of marble and jasper in several colours, it has a pew made of excellent wood at either end.

The Altarpiece

14 metres wide by 26 high, it rises up covering the wall. By Herrera, it is made of marble, jasper and gilded bronze. It is made up of four sections on a strong base. The first section is Doric in style; in the central part it houses the tabernacle by Jácome Trezzo. On the sides are statues in gilded bronze of the four Fathers of the Western Church (St. Jerome, St. Augustine, St. Ambrose and St. Gregory) by León and Pompeyo Leoni, as well as two oil paintings by Tibaldi. The second section is Ionic in style. It contains statues of the four Evangelists, also by León and Pompeyo Leoni, and paintings by Tibaldi and Zuccaro. In the third section, which is Corinthian in style, are figures of St. Andrew and St. James the Elder, by the same sculptors as before, and three more paintings by Zuccaro. Finally, in the top section of the altarpiece is a splendid Calvary with statues of St. Peter and St. Paul on either side. All three are by Pompeyo Leoni and are worked in gilded bronze. This altarpiece cost almost four million reales, twelve maravedies.

15. *The Tabernacle.*

The Tabernacle

This is a real pearl in the main altarpiece as a whole. It is situated within the central columns of the first section of the altarpiece; although actually made by Jácome Trezzo it was conceived and designed by Juan de Herrera. It is in the shape of a circular pavilion; Corinthian in style, the materials used are marble, jasper and gilded bronze.

Eight columns of red jasper streaked with white resting on a jasper base support a finely decorated cornice. On this, coinciding with the columns, are eight pedestals supporting gilded bronze figures of the Apostles. Four other columns in the niches of the intercolumns complete the group of Apostles.

The dome arises from the podium on which these pedestals are placed. A series of bull's eyes runs around the upper part; on the top there is a figure of the Saviour — which is made of the same material as the lower statues and is also the same size. A cylindrical section is within the columns. This is extremely well moulded and has both niches and doors. There is a door at each of the cardinal points; two are open and two are closed with glass.

During the invasion by the French the Tabernacle was taken to pieces and later restored by Manuel de Urquiza, in 1827, by order of Fernando VII. A worse fate befell the valuable monstrance. Made of gold and precious stones, it disappeared during the Napoleonic invasion.

Pieces of Lesser Importance

Among these are the candelabra, especially two large bronze ones: the Corona-

tion, made in Amberes in 1571 by Juan Simón, and the Easter Candelabra, made in the same style by the same person.

Also of note is the Sacrament, lamp made by two famous silversmiths from Madrid in 1833, and the fine marble pulpits at the high altar. With their columns, bannisters and gilded bronze decorations, their richness stands out in the severe sobriety of the basilica as a whole.

The Royal Tombs

These are placed in two large arches which open up on either side of the main chapel. Doric in style, they can be divided into parts: a large base measuring three metres high by eight wide in which there are three doorways, one to the sacristy and reliquaries, the other two to the actual

17. *Felipe II's Cenotaph.*

tombs which, placed on the oratories, make up the second section, which is like a gallery or chapel. In the central part, between the columns, are the groups of worshippers made up of five statues in bronze, copper and gilded brass, which are oversized.

To the left, looking at the altar, is the cenotaph of Carlos V and his family. The armed figure of the emperor, wrapped in the imperial cloak with the impressive figure of a double-headed eagle in black marble, presides over the cenotaph. Carlos V appears at prayer, resting on a cushion in front of the kneeler, his head bare, with Empress Isabel on his right. Behind them is their daughter María, together with Leonor and María, the emperor's sisters.

The scene is completed by an architrave

23

with Ionic columns which surround a large imperial shield with the double-headed eagle and the Golden Fleece. This is topped by another architrave on which is resting a pediment. The materials used are gilded bronze and different shades of marble to produce the heraldic colours.

The cenotaph of Felipe II and his family is to the right, looking at the altar. This complements the previous cenotaph. Felipe II is wearing a cloak with the royal arms worked in coloured marble; on his right is Ana, his fourth wife, and behind him Isabelle de Valois, who was his third wife; on her right is María, Princess of Portugal, who was his first wife and mother of Prince Carlos, who appears her.

The top of the tomb is as on the one previously described, the only difference being that in this case the arms that appear are those of Felipe II and not of Carlos V. These groups are attributed to Pompeyo Leoni because of the style of the figures. If this is so, they make up this artist's greatest work.

Finally of interest is the boveda in the main chapel, with a fresco of the *Coronation of the Virgin* painted by Luchetto, and beside the windows the four major prophets. Other pieces of interest are the reliquaries on the eastern walls of the aisles. These are of different types — glass bells, boxes, small locked boxes, and pavilions. Most are in gilded bronze and date from the time of Felipe II.

The Antechoirs and Choir

The antechoirs are two large rooms situated on either side of the choir. The floors are of marble. Of interest are the frescoes on the vaults, with four stories of David and four of Solomon, all by Lucas Jordán.

The two antechoirs have large arches at the end. These lead to the choir, which is situated over the entrance to the church. Bronze balconies close the choir off from the church. It receives light through several windows which give to the Kings' Courtyard.

The choir stalls, which are Corinthian in style, are made up of two groups of seats, one high and one low, which are separated by a passage-way. They were designed by Juan de Herrera and made under the direction of Italian-born Giuseppe Flecha. The choir stalls are made up of 124 seats all in fine wood (ebony, mahogany, cedar, etc.). The prior's seat deserves special mention, because of its exquisite design.

On the side walls of the choir, above the high stalls, are two Corinthian organs with wooden cases. These are by Master Gil Brevost, an organ builder who was famous throughout Europe at the time of Felipe II.

The frescoes, after drawings by Luchetto, are by Rómulo Cincinato, who also produced the figures decorating the room and the painting in the vault illustrating the *Gloria*.

Finally, two other complementary pieces are worthy of note: the chandelier and the lectern. The former, in rock crystal, is composed of four peacocks with their outspread tails joined in the centre. Above them is an eagle resting on a semi-sphere. Made in Italy it was very badly damaged at the time of the French invasion.

The lectern is on a base of blood-red jasper and white marble on which are placed four pilasters of gilded bronze. The main part is pyramid-shaped, finishing in a cornice. It is topped with a beautiful temple-shaped adornment on a Greek cross.

18. *Jesus Christ, by Benvenuto Cellini. 16th century.* ▶

THE ROYAL PANTHEONS

Felipe II had the idea of building a pantheon, but it was not begun until 1617, during the reign of his son Felipe III. Juan Gómez de Mora, the main architect, directed the work, but it was designed by Juan Bautista Crescenci. The actual building of the pantheon was done by a third person — Pedro de Lizargárate.

At the beginning the work went ahead quickly, but the death of the king in 1621 held it up for 22 years. Problems arose, and the appearance of a leak in the crypt itself led to thoughts about changing its location. A plan by brother Nicolás de Madrid, who was curate there at the time, solved all the problems. The work was thus begun anew in 1645. Alonso Carbonell, the king's chief architect, and Bartolomé Zumbigo, an expert in marble work, were now also involved in the project. The Royal Pantheon was finally inaugurated by Felipe IV on 16th March 1654.

Of particular interest is the staircase leading down to the pantheons. With 34 steps

19. *The Pantheon of the Kings.*

20. *The altar in the Pantheon of the Kings, by Crescenzi, designed by Juan Gómez de Mora.*

a black marble cross by Domenico Guidi.

The chandelier, also Genovese, is by Virgil Fanelli; the angels on the walls holding the candelabra are by Clemente Censore, from Milan.

The sepulchral urns, 24 in all, are in greyish marble and lavish baroque in design. On the front of each is a marble plaque in relief on which can be read the name of the king or queen in question. These plaques are supported by four lion's claws in gilded bronze. To the right of the altar are the king's urns and to the left those of the queens whose sons became kings of Spain, as well as that of Queen Isabel of Borbon, Felipe IV's first wife who was buried here at the express desire of her husband.

Also lying here, between these walls, are Emperor Carlos V, King Felipe II, Felipe III, Felipe IV, Carlos II, Luis I, Carlos III, Carlos IV, Fernando VII, Alfonso XII, Prince Consort Francisco de Asís (the husband of Isabel II) and Alfonso XIII; Empress Isabel and the following queens — Ana, Felipe II's fourth wife; Margarita, Felipe III's wife; Isabel, Felipe IV's first wife; María Ana, Felipe IV's second wife; María Luisa, Felipe V's first wife; María Amalia, Carlos III's wife; María Luisa, Carlos IV's wife; María Cristina, Fernando VII's fourth wife, and Isabel II. Missing are the remains of Felipe V, who

21. *Statue of Juan de Austria lying at rest, by Ponzano and Galleoti.*

is buried in La Granja together with Isabel de Farnesio, his second wife, and of Fernando VI, buried in the Royal de la Salle Church in Madrid, together with his wife Barbara of Braganza.

The Pantheon of the Princes

Commissioned by Isabel II in 1862 to José Segundo de Lema, the palace architect. The work was interrupted in 1868 and recommenced under Alfonso XII, in 1877. It was finished in 1888.

This pantheon is made up of nine burial chambers — five below the sacristy, one below the prior's cell, and three below the chapter houses.

The walls and floors are in magnificent marble from Carrara and Florence; of note are the figures by Ponciano Ponzano and Jacobo Baratta di Leopoldo.

28

The outstanding tombs in the first chamber are that of Princess Luisa Carlota of Borbon, a piece of work by Ponzano and the architect Domingo Gómez de la Puente, that of the Duke and Duchess of Montpensier and those of their daughters Cristina and Amalia. The painting over the altar of *The Descent from the Cross* is by C. Cagliari. Framed in marble it is set in a round moulding of porphyry.

The tomb of Juan of Austria, in white marble from Carrara, is situated in the centre of the fifth chamber. On it lies a statue of him fashioned by Ponzano and made by the Italian sculptor Giuseppe Galeoti.

In the sixth chamber is the mausoleum of the child princes. A polygonal rotunda, it is in poor taste.

THE SACRISTY

The stairs up from the pantheons lead to the ante-sacristy, where there are noteworthy paintings by Nicolás Granello on the vault. The walls in the room are decorated with thirteen paintings given to El Escorial Monastery which depict the *Indulgences;* on the eastern wall there is a fine grey marble fountain, which is beautifully decorated.

The sacristy is a large vaulted room measuring 30 metres long by eight wide. It has a height of eight metres. The room receives light through the eastern wall where there are five large windows in the lower part and nine small ones in the upper part. Also of note are the cupboards made of fine wood, where various religious objects are kept. An extremely beautiful series of drawers made of excellent wood runs the length of the western wall. In the centre is an elegant mirror in silver and rock crystal, donated by Queen María Ana of Austria. The vault, with fine paintings of fabulous scenes, is by Nicolás Granello and Fabrizio Castello.

The sacristy is a large vaulted room meation of paintings, amongst them numerous works by Lucas Jordán. The most outstanding is the one dominating the altar of the Sacred Form, painted by Claudio Coello. It shows the religious ceremony that took place on 19th October 1680 when the Holy Form was solemnly carried to this chapel in the sacristy, and faithfully represents a whole series of important people: King Carlos II, kneeling, worships the Sacred Form, which is being carried by Brother Francisco de los Santos; behind the monarch is Brother Marcos de Herrera and the important members of the Court — the Duke and Duchess of Medinaceli and Pastrana, the Marquis of La Puebla, and so on. In the background come the Hieronymite brothers, singing. The painter himself can also be seen in the foreground on the left, with sideburns. In the upper part are the virtues and angels, holding a curtain. The perspective of the painting should be mentioned as it is very fine, giving the painting a notable depth.

The altar and the sacristy altarpiece are on the southern wall, with a profusion of marble and jasper as well as decorations in gilded bronze. The work is by José del Ol-

mo, Carlos II's architect; the bronze work is by Francesco Filippini. The altar is covered by the painting by Claudio Coello, which is only taken down twice a year; on those two occasions a magnificent Crucifix in gilded bronze by Pietro Tacca can be seen, as well as a large temple-shaped ornament, also in gilded bronze, by Ignacio Millán and Francisco Pecul after a drawing by Vicente López, the royal painter.

THE CHAPTER HOUSES

Leaving the basilica you again enter the porch of the Kings' Courtyard, which leads, on the left, to the old main entrance to the convent, a small vaulted room, known as the Secrets' Room because of its exceptional accoustics which allow visitors to speak to each other in whispers from one corner of the room to the other. This gives to the Trinity Room, so called because of the work by José de Ribera on this subject which formerly hung there. Nowadays it contains a series of paintings by Luchetto, Navarrete, the *Dumb Painter* and Luis de Carvajal.

The chapter houses occupy almost the entire southern corridor of the lower cloisters. They have this name as they were used for the *chapters* or meetings of the Hieronymites. Today they house an art gallery.

The chapter houses are made up of four large consecutive rooms: a central one, which is almost square, containing the entrance door, with two large halls at the sides, known as the Curate's Room and the Prior's Room respectively, and, finally, a smaller room known as the Prior's Lower Cell. All the rooms contain vaults painted with frescoes of fabulous scenes in Renaissance style, with Biblical scenes and saints, by Granello and Fabrizio, the sons of the *Bergamasco,* and by Francisco de Urbino. The frescoes are of splendid decorative effect.

The chapter rooms lead to the main lower cloisters, made up of a spacious covered gallery showing barrel vaults with half-moon shapes. The walls were decorated with large frescoes by Peregrino Tibaldi and his school.

THE MAIN STAIRCASE AND THE EVANGELISTS' COURTYARD

The Main Staircase

This great staircase, which runs from the ground floor to the upper (or processional) cloisters is by Juan Bautista Castello, the *Bergamasco,* and is made up of one section leading to a wide landing where it divides into two. The most interesting thing about it, however, is not the architecture, but the pictorial decoration it has been afforded. Frescoes by Tibaldi and Luchetto, with scenes from the *Life of Christ* decorate its walls. The most important piece of art is, however, by Lucas Jordán, who paint-

◀ 22. *The Sacred Form, by Claudio Coello, 17th century.*

ed the great frieze and the dome during the reign of Carlos II.

The frieze shows the battle, siege and surrender at *San Quintín* on the north, south and west walls, leaving the east wall for the painting of the *foundation of the monastery*. The dome depicts the *Gloria:* in the centre is the Most Holy Trinity; on the right the Virgin Mary with a group of angels carrying the signs of the passion; below is St. Laurence interceding for the King and Queen of Spain; on the left Carlos V, kneeling, is offering a globe, the symbol of the Spanish Empire. Groups of daringly-clad angels surround the central scene and the Theological Virtues are placed at the corners, surrounded by allegorical figures. Finally of note is the scene in which Carlos III, his wife and his mother contemplate the central scene from a balcony.

23. *The main staircase, with panelling by Luchetto and Tibaldi.*

24. *Dome over the main staircase with the Gloria by Lucas Jordán, painted in the 17th century, after the fire in 1671.*

The Evangelists' Courtyard

The lower cloisters encircle the Evangelists' Courtyard, one of Juan de Herrera's most beautiful works. The walls are decorated with two rows of arches, the lower being Doric and the upper Ionic, topped with an elegant balustrade. However the best element is the octagonal pavilion in the centre of the courtyard. Doric in style and covered with a cupola, it also shows a beautiful balustrade. The exterior is of granite, but inside marble combined with jasper has again been used. The four larger walls contain big arches acting as doorways, and the four evangelists together with their symbols. These are by Juan Bautista Monegro in black Geonese marble. Four small ponds, each with a small fountain, surround the pavilion which is in the centre of a beautiful garden with well-cut box trees.

26. *General view of the library.*

THE LIBRARY

Situated over the hallway of the main entrance, which leads to it, the library is in a large room measuring 45 metres long by nine wide and ten high. Covered with a barrel vault, the floor is in white and greyish marble. Beautiful Doric shelving runs along its walls. Designed by Juan de Herrera and made by Flecha, Gamboa, Serrano and other masters, it is made of excellent woods on a marble base.

In the centre of the room is a globe made in Florence in 1536, together with five marble and bronze tables dating from the foundation of the monastery. Among them stand two eight-sided porphyry candlesticks donated by Felipe IV.

27. *José de Sgüenza, the first chronicler of the monastery.*

Of the paintings in this room the most important are the life-size portraits of Carlos V, Felipe II and Felipe III, painted by Juan Pantoja de la Cruz, and that of Carlos II by Juan Carreño de Miranda.

The wall above the shelving and the vault are painted with frescoes; these are great compositions alluding to arts and sciences. The vault is divided into seven sections, where Peregrino Tibaldi depicted the liberal arts as Roman matrons; in the space between the bookshelves and the cornice is a true frieze with scenes alluding to the same liberal arts.

The two central points of the walls are given over to representations of Philosophy and Theology, with corresponding stories on the frieze: the *School in Athens* and the *Council of Nicaea* respectively. The paintings are completed with Renaissance fabulous scenes which are of great fantasy and beauty. Tibaldi was aided in his work on these paintings by members of his school, in particular by Bartolomé Carducci and Francisco de Viana.

Of real importance among the texts kept in this library are: St. John's *Apocalypse* from the 13th century; a Roman missal from the 15th century; Isabel la Católica's prayer book; the breviaries belonging to Carlos V and Felipe II, both with beautifully illuminated pages, Arabic and Persian books which are sumptuously adorned in oriental style; the *Apocalypse* by Beato de Liébana, from the 9th century; the *Golden Codex* from 1043; the Holy Bible, from the 14th century; the *Trojan Chronicle* from the 14th century; Ptolomy's *Cosmography* and numerous works by famous writers such as Cicero, Virgil,

28. *Miniatures from a page of the Cantigas (poetry to be set to music) by Alfonso X, the Wise King.*

29. *Miniatures from a page of the Albelde de Iregua Codex.*

Horace, Titus Livius, St. Theresa of Avila, and so on.

To the 4,000 books brought by Felipe II was joined the collection of Italian books donated by Ambassador Diego Hurtado de Mendoza. Later added, by order of Felipe II, were 130 from the Royal Chapel in Granada, which had belonged to the Kings of Castile; 94 from the Bishop of Plasencia; 234 from Jerónimo de Zurita; 87 from Doctor Páez de Castro; 239 from Mallorca, Barcelona and other monasteries, together with those from Raimundo Lulio; 31 from the Prior of Roncesvalles; 139 from the Inquisition; 206 from Arias Montano; 45 from Alonso de Zúñiga; 486 from the Marquis of Vélez; 933 from Bobadilla y Mendoza, the Cardinal of Burgos; and 135 from the Archbishop of Tarragona, as well as various donations of Greek, Hebrew and Arabic manuscripts. Of the 1,051 Hellenic manuscripts kept in Spain, 586 are to be found in El Escorial monastery, catalogued by Arias Montano and José de Sigüenza, as are the rest of the texts in this library.

30. *Benito Arias Montano.*

THE PALACE OF THE BORBONS

The House of Austria made of the monastery of San Lorenzo the pre-eminent royal palace by spending long periods in it. With the arrival of the House of Borbon it had to share its primacy with La Granja, El Pardo and Aranjuez, but under Carlos III and his son Carlos IV it regained the position which it had previously enjoyed.

The ensemble of decorative pieces such as furniture, chandeliers, clocks and other items is of great value, but the most important is the collection of tapestries, numbering more than 200. Many of the ceilings are decorated with paintings by Felipe López, in Pompeian style, which was typical at the time of the Spanish empire and is well-represented in this palace.

The palace is entered by the north façade leading directly onto the 18th century staircase by Villanueva.

31. *Corner of the Pompeian drawing room. The Palace of the Borbons.*

Then three small rooms lead to what is in fact the Palace of the Borbons. They contain elegant neo-classic and imperial style furniture together with paintings by Maella and other artists.

The following room is that known as the Chinese Room, as it houses some exquisite crockery in Chinese porcelain. This room leads directly to those known as the King's Rooms, meaning Carlos IV's rooms which have a marked official character. The first is the Official Dining Room, a large room with some excellent tapestries designed by Goya, Bayeu, Castillo and Anglois.

The chairs are imperial in style; elegant clocks and cut glass chandeliers complete the decoration. This dining room is followed by a small drawing room and the Ambassadors Antechamber, with several tapestries designed by Goya, and then by the Ambassadors' Room. Here too is a good collection of tapestries, this time by Bayeu. Equally worthy of mention is the imperial-

32. *The King's Rooms. Detail of one of the rooms with 18th century tapestries.*

style furniture and the Sèvres vases which decorate the room.

From the room known as the Oratory, containing tapestries with scenes from the *Story of Telemacos,* you enter those known as the Queen's Rooms, referring to Queen María Luisa, wife of Carlos IV. The first contains tapestries, again with pieces showing the adventures of Telemacos, Ulysses' son, and imperial-style furniture. The second room is decorated with tapestries by Anglois and leads to the Pompeian-style Room, given this name because of the beautiful tapestries decorating it.

◄ **33.** *"The Kite". Tapestry designed by Goya, 18th century.*

34. *A hunting scene, after Wouwerman, in one of the rooms in the palace.*

35. *Pedro Rico, the sausage seller, a tapestry designed by Bayeu. The Amabassadors' Room.*

They were woven in the Santa Bárbara workshop and the designs are by José del Castillo. Two other small rooms lead to the final one in this 18th century Palace — the Teniers Tapestry room, which houses copies produced in the Royal Workshop in Madrid.

Parallel to all the rooms which have just been described are those which were the monarchs' private rooms and the so-called *wood* rooms. Notable among these is the Reception Room, with romantic-style furniture, an elegant chandelier in bronze and glass and containing a beautiful black marble fireplace. The *wood* rooms are a fine example of carpentry and tracery in excellent woods such as ebony lignum vitae, cedar and others.

36. *Neptune. Tapestry on a design attributed to Rubens, in one of the Queen's Rooms.*

37. *The Battle Room. The 16th century vault, in Pompeian style, is by Lázaro Tavarón and Orazio Cambiasso.*

The Battle Room

Between the Palace of the House of Borbon and that of the House of the Austrias is the Battle Room, so called because the walls are decorated with frescoes depicting the most famous victories for the Castilian and Spanish armies at different times in history. On the southern wall is a fresco by Granelo, Castello and Tavarón depicting *The Battle of La Higueruela*, where Juan II of Castile beat the Arabs from Granada in 1431. On the side walls are the two victorious *Expeditions to the Azores* by Felipe II's fleet, painted by Granelo, and on the nothern wall are various scenes from The Battle and the Taking of San Quintín, by Castello, and scenes of squares in France and Flanders, painted by Garnello and Tavarón.

This room was restored at the end of the 19th century by Rudesindo Marín and his sons, with the collaboration of José de Lerma, the architect who also designed the iron railing.

38. *Detail from The Battle of La Higueruela.* ▶

THE SIXTEENTH CENTURY PALACE

The austerity of the 16th century palace contrasts greatly with the richness and luxury of the Borbon palace. The rooms used by Felipe II and his family constitute living evidence to the humility of the man who was the most powerful in the world at the time.

His rooms are distributed around the main chapel of the church and the part known as the Masks Courtyard, because of the two fountains with water pouring from stone masks. A stone stairway leads down from the Battle Room through some cloisters, like a gallery, with oil paintings by Castello and Pantoja de la Cruz to the

rooms which were first known as the Queen's Room, but now as the rooms of Princess Isabel Clara Eugenia, Felipe II's favourite daughter. Of interest in this room are the walnut bed, with curtains and canopy in oriental style, a claviorgan which belonged to Carlos V and an ivory figure of Christ by Alonso Cano, as well as the numerous paintings hanging on the walls.

A passage running over the vault in the Royal Pantheon and to the back of the high altar leads to Felipe II's rooms. Perhaps the most outstanding of these is the bedroom (where a door giving to the church enabled the monarch to hear the

39. *Felipe II's rooms in the 16th century palace.*

40. *The rooms used by Princess Isabel Clara Eugenia, Felipe II's daughter.*

services from his bed) and the office, a large, extremely austere room with a brick floor and walls and vaults painted in white. The only decoration is the lower part of the walls, with painted tiles from Talavera. The furniture is also sober. The most interesting of the paintings are a portrait of Felipe II as an old man, by Pantoja de la Cruz, a panel from the Flemish school with *The Presentation of the Virgin in the Temple*, and *The Transfiguration on Mount Tabor*, after Raphael.

Another passage leads to the Walk Gallery and to the Antechamber, or Ambassadors' Room. In this room hang various views of royal residences and hunting lodges, such as El Pardo and Aranjuez, and prints by Pierre Perret showing different parts of the monastery as drawn by Juan de Herrera.

The Walk Gallery is decorated with a collection of paintings commemorating Spanish victories in France and Flanders during the reign of Felipe II, the most interesting being that of the battle of San Quintín, an old painting by Castello and Granello, two brothers.

This leads to the room which is known

as the Portrait Room because of the paintings it houses. Among them are portraits of Carlos V, painted by Pantoja de la Cruz in 1547; of Felipe II by Antonio Moro; of Felipe III by Pantoja; of Felipe IV as a child, painted by Bartolomé González in 1612; and a portrait of Carlos II, by Carreño. The last room is called the Sedan Chair Room, as this is the most important piece it contains. This chair was used by Felipe II; in it he made his last journey from Madrid to El Escorial before his death. The most important of the paintings in the room are the four by Jacobo Bassano.

41. *The Garden of Delights, a tapestry after the painting of the same name by El Bosco.*

THE ART GALLERY

The National Heritage, the organisation in charge of Palaces and Royal Residences, considered it necessary to change the siting of the large collection of paintings which had always been exhibited in the Chapter Houses and the Sacristy. These rooms did not meet the minimum requirements for the exhibition of paintings as they are quite small and do not receive sufficient light. For this reason it was decided that Felipe II's Summer Palace should be restored and used as the monastery art gallery.

50

The greater part of the collection is made up of 15th and 16th century works in Renaissance style, together with a fair number of 17th century Baroque paintings.

The 15th and 16th century Flemish and German schools are represented by works such as *Landscape with St. Christopher* by Joaquín Patinir; *The Creation,* a part of *The Garden of Delights and Insults* by El Bosco; *Studies in Natural History* by Durero, and Gerard David's *Triptych* with *The Pietà, John the Baptist and St. Francis.* The manieristic style, the final detail of the Renaissance in the second half of 16th century, is highly represented within the Flemish school by Miguel Coccie's works: *Triptich of the Story of St. Philip, The Annunciation, Virgin with Child* and *St. Joachim and St. Ann.* Also of interest is the copy by the same painter of the *Descent from the Cross* by Roger van der Weyden.

Also present are the following paintings from the 16th century Italian school, in particular from the Venetian school: *The Last Supper* and *John the Baptist* by Titian; a good collection of works by Tintoretto, such as *Mary Magdalen, Penitent, The Burial of Christ, The Nativity with the Adoration of the Shepherds;* some magnificent works by Verones, such as *The Annunciation, The Apparition of Christ before His Mother, God the Father and the Holy Spirit.* Finally, there are paintings by Vaccaro, Bassano, Guido Reni and Zuccaro.

The 17th century works are basically from the Spanish school. José de Ribera is represented by his *St. Jerome, Penitent, St. Francis, St. Paul* and *The Burial of Christ.* Of particular interest among the works by José de Ribera and by lesser members of his

42. *The Adoration of the Shepherds by Tintoretto, 16th century.*

43. *"Calvary" by Roger van der Weyden, 15th century.*

school is a magnificent piece, *Joseph's Coat*, painted by Diego de Velázquez during his period in Rome in 1630, as well as *The Birth of the Virgin* by Valdés Leal. Representative of Flemish baroque is *The Supper at Emmaus*, by Rubens, a sketch for the final painting which is kept in the Prado Museum.

The most outstanding of all the works in the collection are the painting by Velázquez cited above, together with the following: *The Martyrdom of St. Maurice*, a masterpiece by Domenico Theotocopuli, El Greco, the most important work in El Escorial. It depicts the execution of the

Theban Legion and their leader. St. Maurice, by order of the Roman Emperor Maximianus Hercules after their refusal to take part in the sacrifices to the gods decreed by the emperor, who had gone with his legion to put down the Gauls that were in revolt.

Calvary by Roger van der Weyden.

Tapestry from the series depicting the *Conquest of Tunisia* by Wilhelm Pannemaker, woven in gold; silver and silk, and completed in 1554.

The final pieces are a stained-glass window with Carlos V's sword and gorget, and various documents referring to the monastery and the king, such as the letter signed by Felipe II to his father, informing him of the victory in the battle of San Quintín.

44. *The Creation, part of The Garden of Delights by El Bosco. 15th century.*

EL GRECO
EL SUEÑO DE FELIPE II

45. *Adoration of the Name of Jesus or Felipe II's Dream by El Greco. 16th century.*

46. *The Martyrdom of St. Maurice by El Greco. 16th century.* ▶

THE MUSEUM OF ARCHITECTURE

Situated in the basement of the Summer Palace, the Museum of Architecture is made up of the following rooms:

ROOM I

This room contains a description of the works of the artists with paintings in the monastery, from Juan de Herrera through El Greco and Pompeyo Leoni to Benito Arias Montano.

ROOM II

Contains details of the different costs of building the monastery and the total sum spent on its construction, as well as outlines of the general organisation of the architectural work and of its financing. It also contains the payrolls and the daily record of the works, signed by Brother Juan de San Jerónimo.

ROOMS III AND IV

A considerable number of plans, layouts and designs by Juan de Herrera can be seen in room III; room IV contains prints by Pierre Perret based on Herrera's designs.

ROOM V

Contains reproductions of pictures of the monastery arranged according to the different periods and artists, from that painted in Amberes in 1602, to that painted in Amsterdam in 1741, as well as some other recent works.

ROOM VI

Contains pictures of the monastery dating from its foundation as well as some later ones, such as the scene by the Dutch painter Swanenburgh from the 16th century, or the paintings by Fernando Brambilla from the 19th century, and a wooden model of the monastery.

ROOM VII

Contains several interesting collections of tools used in the building of the monastery, such as trowels, drills, templates and so on.

ROOM VIII

Contains the principal materials used in the construction of the monastery: granite, ceramics, slate, and so on.

ROOMS IX, X AND XI

The first of these rooms contains examples of carpentry and woodwork; the second contains examples of different skills used in the work, with collections of work by locksmiths, ironsmiths, silversmiths and goldsmiths, together with glasswork and plumbing work.

Room XI contains examples of different machines invented by Herrera for the construction of the Royal Monastery, like the famous quill, a real crane (a wooden model of which, dating from the time of the construction of the monastery, still exists), or very large pliers which were used to raise the blocks of stone.

47. Dining Room in the Prince's Home, designed by Villanueva in the 18th century. ▶

THE PRINCE'S VILLA

This was built by Juan de Villanueva in 1772 at the express wish of Carlos, Prince of Asturias (later King Carlos IV) to be used as a small palace for his recreation, It is built in the shape of a "T", made up of a central tower with an arm coming from each of three of its sides.

The main façade, which consists of three sections, is extremely sober, the only decorative elements being some simple ledges and window decorations on the lower floor, and a slightly-projecting cornice on the upper floor. The most outstanding feature is an elegant central colonnade made up of Tuscany columns which support a simple entablature. This, surrounded by an iron railing, forms a wide balcony which projects beyond the cornice. The smaller west façade also contains a small central porch supported by Tuscany columns.

The interior is composed of several rooms, most of which are quite small. They are neo-classic and imperial in style and are richly hung with silk brocades from the times of Carlos IV and Fernando VII. The vaults, most of which are painted in Pompeian style, are by Juan Duque, Jacinto Gómez Pastor, Manuel Pérez and Felipe López; the gilt stucco work is by Ferroni and the Brilli brothers. Most of the floors are paved in black and white marble, although the staircase is made of coloured marble and jasper. The best floors are in the rooms *worked in excellent wood* which contain some extremely beautiful examples of marquetry and inlay work, all in the highest quality materials.

The first room in the house is the hall, which leads to another containing an excellent collection of paintings by Lucas Jordán, depicting mythological as well as historical and religious scenes. A second room houses numerous paintings of flower vases and still life scenes, the most interesting being *The Water Melon* by López Enguidanos. The third room contains more works by Lucas Jordán; in fact a large number of paintings by this artist are to be found in this house.

A further room leads to the Dining Room, the largest room in the house, and one of the most magnificent. Hung with green satin, it contains numerous pictures by Lucas Jordán, the most important of which are *The Death of Julian the Apostate* and *The Conversion of St. Paul*.

The furniture is imperial in style; of particular interest is the large central table which has 16 columns with Corinthian capitals in gilded bronze supporting a mahogany top with marble mosaic work. A magnificent gilded bronze and glass chandelier with 48 lights completes the decoration of this room.

The following room is the Coffee Room. Oval in shape, it contains four niches each with a marble bust of a Roman emperor. On the central pedestal table stands an alabaster temple-shaped ornament containing a bust of Fernando VII.

The rooms on the right-hand side of the house an ample collection of works by Corrado Giaquinto, with paintings on religious, mythological and allegorical themes.

THE UPPER VILLA

This was commissioned by Prince Gabriel of Borbon, brother to Carlos IV. The architect employed was again Juan Villanueva; this house is smaller and more simple than the Prince's Villa.

Square in shape, the main façade contains a porch with Ionic columns and a complex crown, marked by the sober, elegant style of Villanueva.

The rooms are laid out around a central room which may have been a Music Room.

This villa was used as a summer residence up to the time of Fernando VII, and is set in a garden with ornamental box-trees.

FURTHER PLACES OF INTEREST

The most important of the other places to visit outside the monastery and the villas is the María Cristina University beyond the Convalescents' Gallery. This building by Herrera is run by the Order of St. Augustine, who took over from the Hieronymites in 1885 and has since then been in charge of the religious, university and cultural duties and of the conservation of the basilica, the University and the Alfonso XII school. A garden dominated by a statue of Felipe II, like the one in Terreros Park, lies before the main door; it is often used for walks and conversations. The park also contains a statue in honour of the *carabineros*, a military corps which had schools and academies in El Escorial, as did previously the Bodyguards and the Royal Guard.

Some façades and interiors of the palaces constructed by the nobility in the town created by Carlos III and Carlos IV when they founded the Royal Seat of San Lorenzo at a short distance from the town of El Escorial at the end of the 18th century still remain.

49. *Gardens of the María Cristina University, founded in 1885.*

Designed by Juan de Villanueva, architect to both these kings, they include: *The Consul's House* in Juan de Leiva Street; *The Princes' House* on the hill leading to the station, residence of Prince Francisco de Paula, brother to Fernando VII, now in ruins, but admirable because of the harmony of the stonework; *Carlos III's Royal Coliseum,* the only baroque court theatre that exists in Spain (it is still used), built by a French architect — Marquet — in 1770, with innovations by Villanueva in 1774, and finally restored in 1979, completely maintaining its old aspect of the day on which it was inaugurated by Carlos III; the *old fortress and prison in Pozas Street,* magnificently converted and used as a Senior Citizens' centre; the *Palace of Mon-*

tejovellar with its balconies can still be seen in San Antón Street and Animas Square, as can the façades of the *Palaces of the Dukes of Alba and Medinaceli,* though those of Godoy, Osuna and other nobles have unfortunately disappeared.

Likewise, evocative corners and streets with features from centuries gone by are still to be found, such as the *Market Corner* on Medinaceli Street with Flower Hill. In *Animas Square* you can almost breathe the 18th century; in *Cruz Street,* also known as *Las Tiendas Street* there is a fountain decorated with a cross and some arcades from the 19th century with stone columns erected in the 18th which are almost as well known as the monastery itself, due to the number of people who congregate there; the *cottage* over the Romeral dam; the modern Felipe II Hotel, on one side of the dam, a building which was and still is a meeting place for famous people from both Spain and abroad, now converted into a university centre and a residence for students and lecturers from universities in the USA; *St. Bernabé's church,* built in 1595, in which are buried several artists who took part in the decoration of the mon-

50. *View of the rear part of the Administration Offices, by Herrera.*

61

51. *St. Bernabé's church. 16th century.*

52. *Carlos III's Royal Coliseum. 18th century.*

astery — Luqueto, Urbino, Granello, and Miguel Antona or Azcona, the court jester; the latter's old house, used by Felipe II while the monastery was being built; *Granjilla Palace* and houses in different parts of the town of El Escorial which were in ruins and have now been restored.

Floridablanca Street is the one which shows the development of architecture in the 18th century, as opposed to the Herrera style used in the 16th century. Of interest in the second style are the *Administration Offices,* built by Herrera as offices for Felipe II's administrative staff; these were finished by Villanueva in the 18th century and joined to other offices by means of direct communication through underground and above ground passageways from the Borbons Palace to the Carlos III Theatre. In the second Administration Offices, in the courtyard to the left of the gardens in Benavente Square, with its monument dedicated to Crispin, a character from *Created Interest,* there is a granite plaque from the people of San Lorenzo to Ortega y Gasset, who lived in this house and in it wrote his first book, *Meditations on Don Quixote.*

53. *Las Tiendas Street, a very old street with porticos dating from the 19th century.*

54. *Constitution Square, with the Town Hall.*

55. *La Virgen de Gracia hermitage in La Herrería.*

57. *The Princes' Villa, residence of Prince Francisco de Paula, brother to Fernando VII.*▶

◄ **56.** *Floridablanca Street.*

58. *Benavente Square.*

59. *Portrait of Carlos V as a young man, by Juan Pantoja de la Cruz.*

The first main fact in a simple summary of the events which took place in El Escorial throughout 400 years, from Felipe II to Alfonso XIII, is that Felipe II spent fourteen years in the palace, not counting his holiday visits. The mortal remains of his father, Emperor Carlos V, were taken from Yuste monastery to El Escorial, where they were laid to rest in the chapel of the Old, or *Prestado* church (closed to the public), where the Hieronymites held their church services during the construction of the basilica. In this church was the former Royal Pantheon (situated under the altar) and an outstanding painting by Titian of *The Martyrdom of St. Laurence.* There the king received news of the victory at Lepanto. In the palace he organised the difficult business in Flanders; there he was informed of the death of King Sebastian of Portugal, whom he esteemed most highly, and of his half-brother, Juan de Austria. Surrounded by Hieronymite monks, counsellors and soldiers, he administered justice, promoted culture, and carried out a policy which was correct in his time — the conquest of the Philippines, the evangelization of America, the naval disaster of the Invicible Armada, wars against foreign enemies. The good and the bad in a kingdom where the sun never set.

Felipe III began the construction of the Royal Pantheon envisaged by his father; he placed the bronze statues on the tombs of Carlos V and Felipe II. Villacastin-Sigüenza died (as did Herrera in 1597). The library of Muley Zidán, Emperor of Morocco, made up of 4,000 volumes of books as well as Arabic, Turkish and Persian manuscripts increased the content of the royal library.

The pantheon, designed by Italian-born Crescenzi and built by Brother Nicolás de Madrid, was completed during the reign of Felipe IV, The royal bodies were carried to their new resting place in an impressive ceremony. In 1649 the monastery was lit up with 1,200 lights to receive Mariana of Austria, the king's second wife. A valuable collection of paintings was hung in the sacristy.

During the reign of Carlos II, who first

60. *Portrait of Felipe II, by Juan Pantoja de la Cruz.*

61. *Portrait of Felipe IV.*

visited the monastery in 1676, the altar of the Sacred Form was rebuilt. Lucas Jordán painted the vault over the main staircase in the monastery.

During the reigns of Felipe V and Fernando VI the interior cloisters were closed with framed windows. During those of Carlos III and Carlos IV courtly life was renewed, the town of San Lorenzo, the Prince's Villa and the Upper Villa were created, as was the portico separating the two villages. Villanueva constructed the main staircase in the Borbons Palace, where outstanding works of art were kept. Prince Fernando was imprisoned for having conspired against his father, Carlos IV.

During the reign of Fernando VII the French sacked the monastery, but the altarpiece, the tabernacle and the figure of Christ by Cellini were recuperated in 1814. Marble pulpits were built in the basilica, with columns and adornments in gilded bronze — medallions with the four fathers of the Church.

During the reign of Isabel II the princes' pantheon was inaugurated. The Hieronymites left the monastery, to be replaced by the Escolapians. In the reign of Alfonso XII custody of the monastery was handed over to the Augustine monastic order. When Queen María Cristina was regent the Alfonso XII school and the María Cristina University were founded in the old Campaña building. Later, in 1980 and 1985 the mortal remains of Alfonso XIII and of his wife, Queen Victoria Eugenia, were laid to rest in the royal pantheon.

INDEX

THE SPANISH NATIONAL HERITAGE COLLECTION

El Escorial
Los Caídos Valley
Las Huelgas Royal Monastery
The Royal Palace in Madrid
La Almudaina Palace

INDEX

Page

Historical Introduction 5
The Outside of El Escorial Monastery 8
    The West façade 9
    The South façade 9
    The North façade 14
    The East façade 14
    The Dome 14
The Kings' Courtyard 15
The Basilica 18
    The Altarpiece 20
    The Tabernacle 21
    Pieces of lesser importance 21
    The Royal tombs 22
    The Antechoirs and choir 24
The Royal pantheons 26
    The Pantheon of the kings 27
    The Pantheon of the princes 28
The Sacristy 29
The Chapter houses 31
The Main staircase and the Evangelists' courtyard 31
    The Main staircase 31
    The Evangelists' courtyard 34
The Library 35
The Palace of the Borbons 39
    The Battle room 45
The 16th century palace 48
    The Art gallery 50
    The Museum of architecture 56
    The Prince's Villa 57
    The Upper Villa 59
    Further places of interest 59
    Monarchs in El Escorial 67